Best Start

MUSIC LESSONS

SONG BOOK 2

for
Recorder
Fife
Flute

by Sarah Broughton Stalbow

Best Start Publishing
www.beststartmusic.com

First published in 2019 by Best Start Publishing

© Sarah Broughton Stalbow, 2019

ISBN: 978-0-6485764-3-3

The moral rights of the author have been asserted.

All rights reserved. Except as permitted under the Australian Copyright Act 1968 (for example, a fair dealing for the purposes of study, research, criticism or review), no part of this book may be reproduced, stored in a retrieval system, communicated or transmitted in any form or by any means without prior written permission.

All inquiries should be made to the author.

All musical compositions by Sarah Broughton Stalbow, except for the following by Dominic G. Harvey: page 26 *Jammin'* and page 28 *Brubeck Eski* .

Cover art and text design by Sarah Broughton Stalbow, editing by Rob Stalbow.

A catalogue record for this book is available from the National Library of Australia

Best Start Publishing
www.beststartmusic.com

Audio tracks for songs are available at:

www.beststartmusic.com/backingtracks

Every song has a short instrumental introduction.

Stream them for free anytime and play along!

Piano accompaniments are available in the Best Start Music Lessons Book 2: For Teachers.

Available from **www.beststartmusic.com** and on Amazon.

Remember to always:

> **Clap Sing Play**
>
> First: clap the rhythm.
> Next: sing the note names.
> Then: play it!

Reading Music

Music notes are written on 5 lines and 4 spaces - this is called the STAFF or STAVE.

You can remember the notes on the LINES like this:

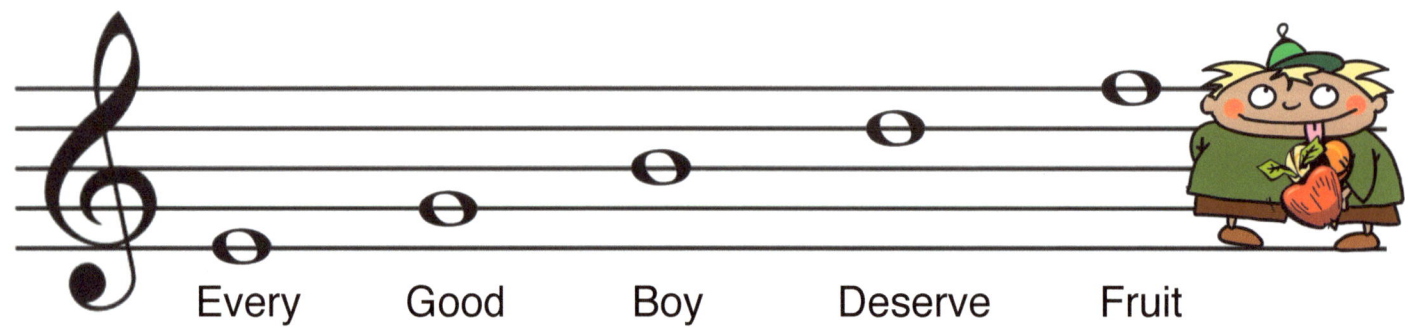

Every   Good   Boy   Deserve   Fruit

You can remember the notes in the SPACES like this:

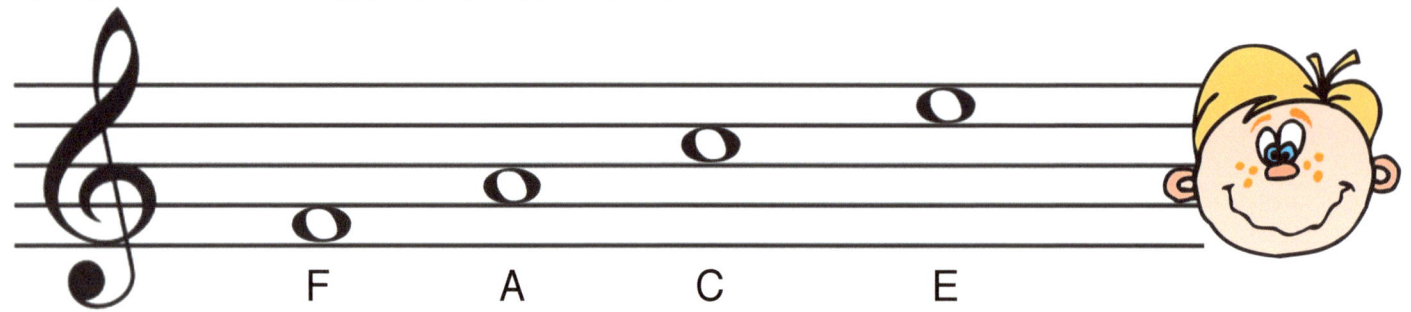

F   A   C   E

Notes in this book

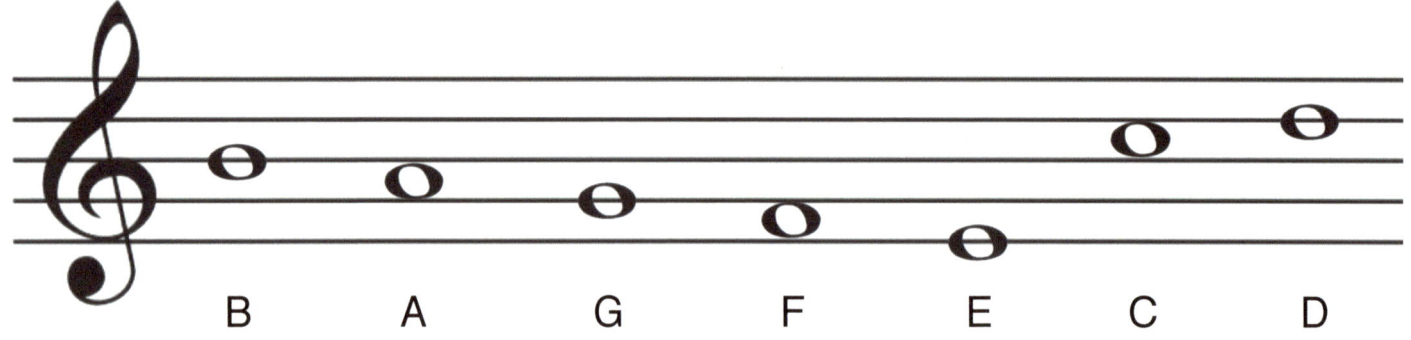

B   A   G   F   E   C   D

Rhythms in this book

Symbol	Rhythm name	Notation name	Value
♩	Ta	Crotchet or Quarter Note	1 beat
♩ (half note)	Ta-a	Minim or Half Note	2 beats
♩. (dotted half)	Ta-a-a	Dotted Minim or Dotted Half Note	3 beats
o	Great Big Whole Note	Semibreve or Whole Note	4 beats
♫	Ti-ti (Tee-tee)	Quavers or Eighth Notes	1/2 a beat each (one beat together)
♬♬	Tika-tika	Semiquavers or Sixteenth Notes	1/4 of a beat each (one beat together)

  Recorder  Fife / Flute

 Recorder 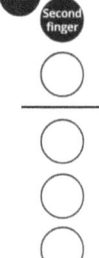 Fife / Flute

 Recorder      Fife / Flute

C
 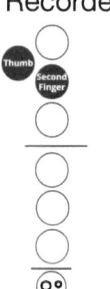 

E
 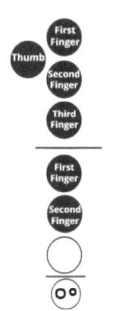 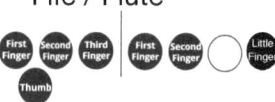

F
 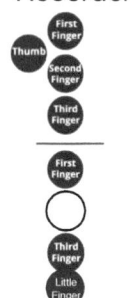 

D

Warm ups

1. Long notes

2. Slurred octaves - up

For flute

3. Slurred octaves - down

For flute

Mini scales

Play ALL TONGUED and then ALL SLURRED.

Tick the boxes when you can play them from memory.

1. Groove Machine

Wait for the 8 bar introduction.

Point to the staccato notes and play them first.

Wait for an 8 bar instrumental break.

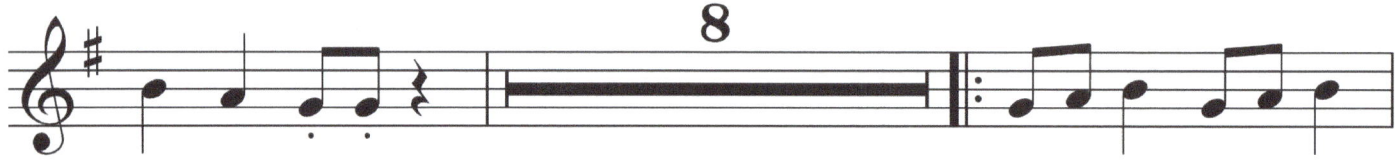

Don't forget the repeat!

2. Twilight Lullaby

Wait for the 4 bar introduction, then play.

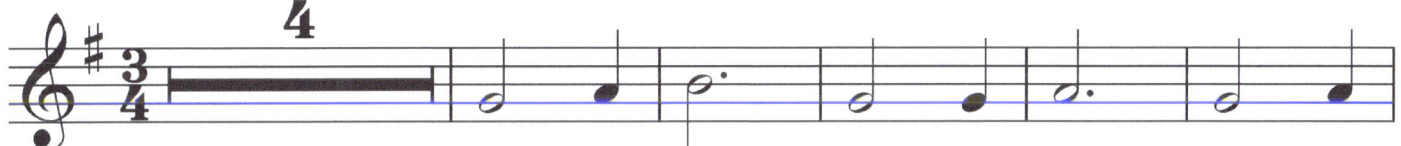

Wait for the 4 bar instrumental break.

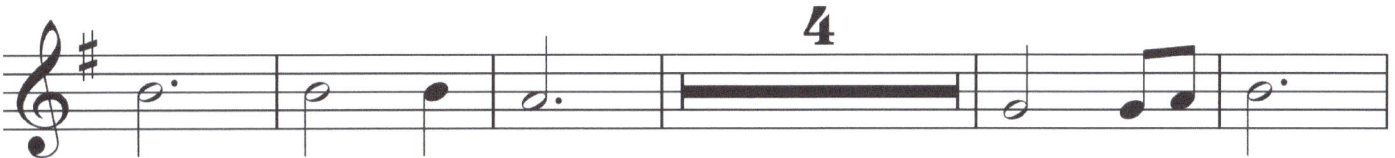

molto rit

3. Gliding

Wait for the 8 bar introduction.

Notice the slurs in this song and play them first.

This means one whole bar rest.

Wait for the instrumental break, and then play it again.

4. Paradise

Wait for an 8 bar introduction, then play.   Point to the two beat rests.

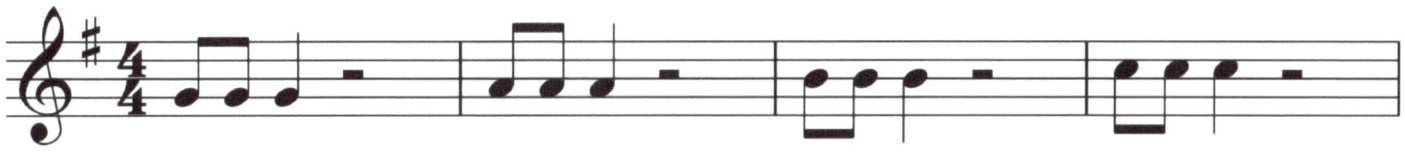

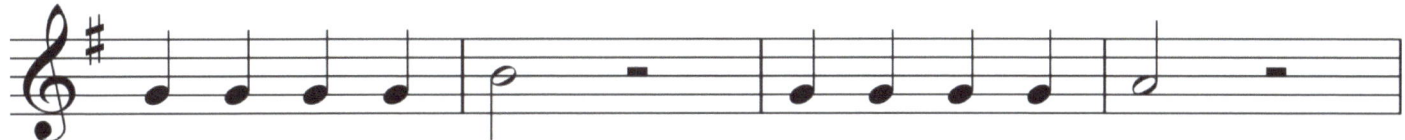

Go back to the beginning and play it all again!
Keep repeating until the music stops.

5. Gently

Wait for an 8 bar introduction, then play.

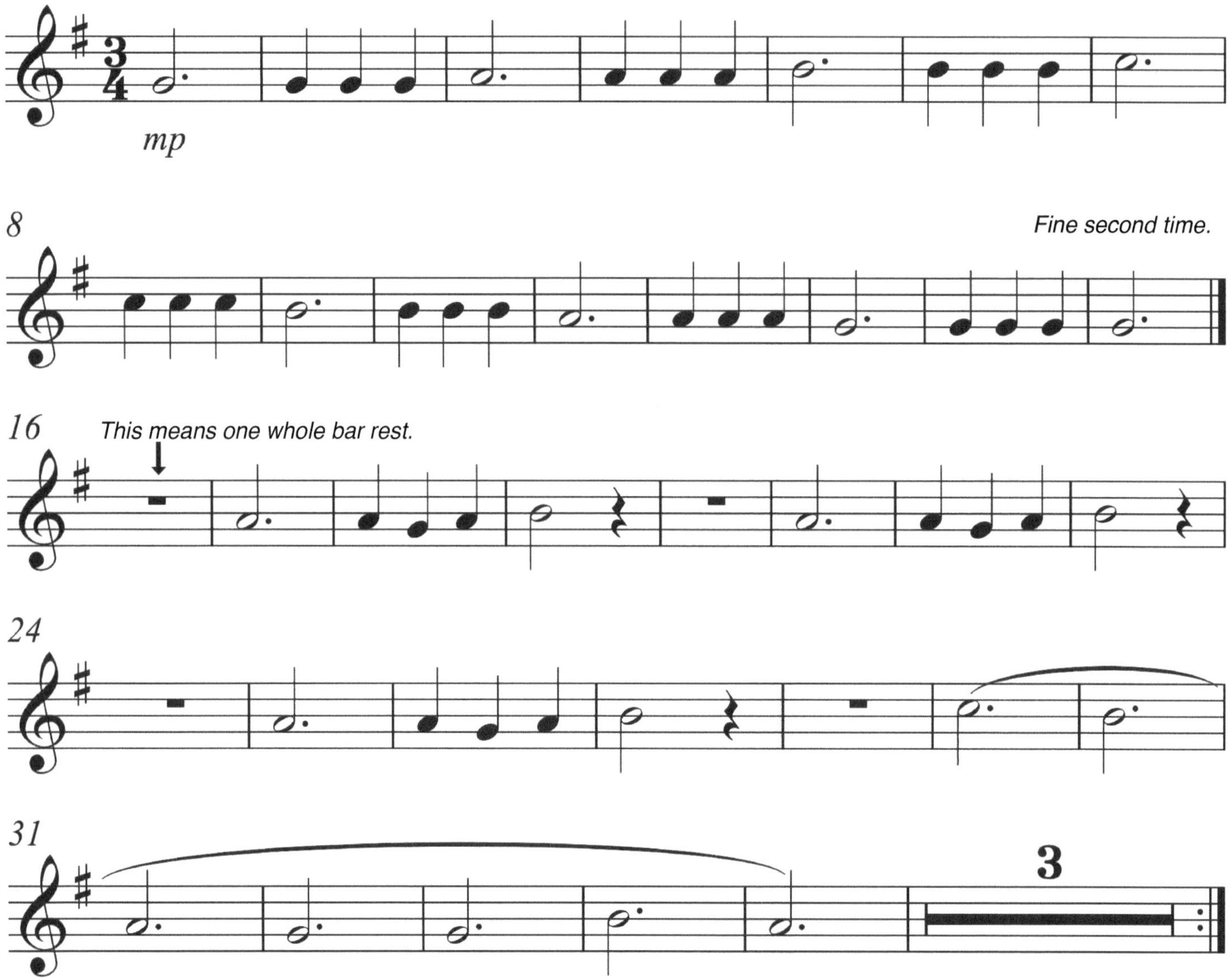

Check the time signature, how many beats are in each bar? You will need to count the rests!

Fine second time.

This means one whole bar rest.

Wait for the 3 bar instrumental, then go back to the beginning and finish at "Fine" (Italian for "finish"!)

6. Orange Juice

Notice the dynamic markings.
What do they mean?

7. The Elephant and the Grasshopper

Wait for a 2 bar introduction, then play.

The dynmics are very important in this song!

8. Red Moon

Wait for the 3 bar introduction, then play.

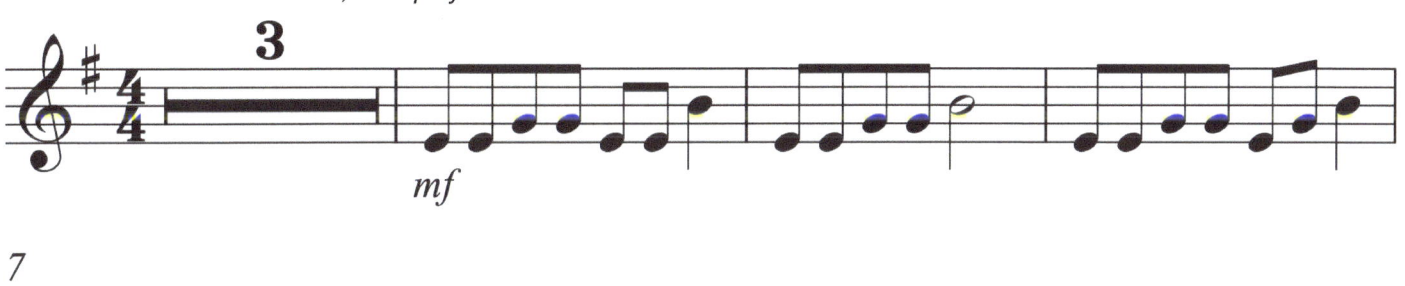

(This is the same tune as the beginning!)

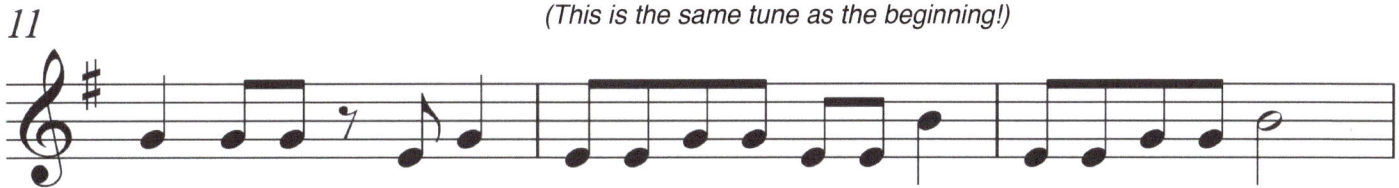

9. Drifting

Can you find STEPS and SKIPS in this song?
Hint: Steps are notes that are right next to each other.
Skips will skip over their neighbour.

Wait for an 8 bar introduction.

*Wait for an 8 bar instrumental break,
then play it again!*

10. Boot Scootin' Betty

Wait for a 4 bar introduction.

mf

Wait for the 8 bar instrumental, then play the tune again.

11. My Pet Llama

Wait for the 4 bar introduction.

12. Calm Chameleon

You can play this as a duet with your teacher.

13. Fossil Fenzy

Wait for a 1 bar introduction.

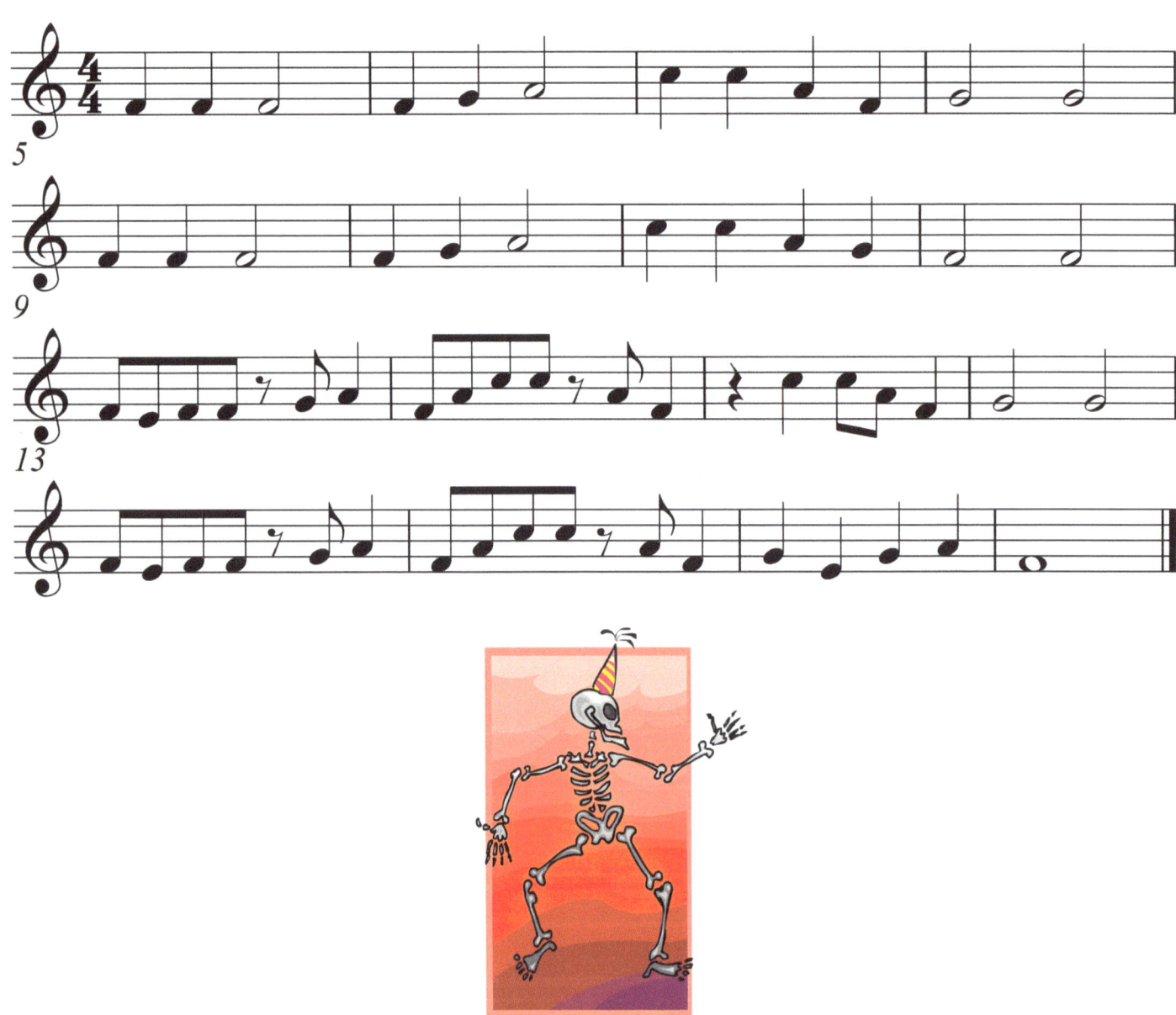

14. Feel the Beat

Wait for a 1 bar introduction.   Find the tika-tikas and play them.

15. Walk the Dog

A TIE is a curved line that joins notes that are the same pitch. Hold for the value of both notes.

Wait for the 3 bar introduction.

Find the bars with tied notes and play them.

16. Morning Song

Wait for a 2 bar introduction.

17. Sunrise

Wait for 1 bar introduction.

18. Silver Starlight

You can play this song as a duet with your teacher.

Learn the top part first. When you are comfortable with the rhythm, learn the bottom part.

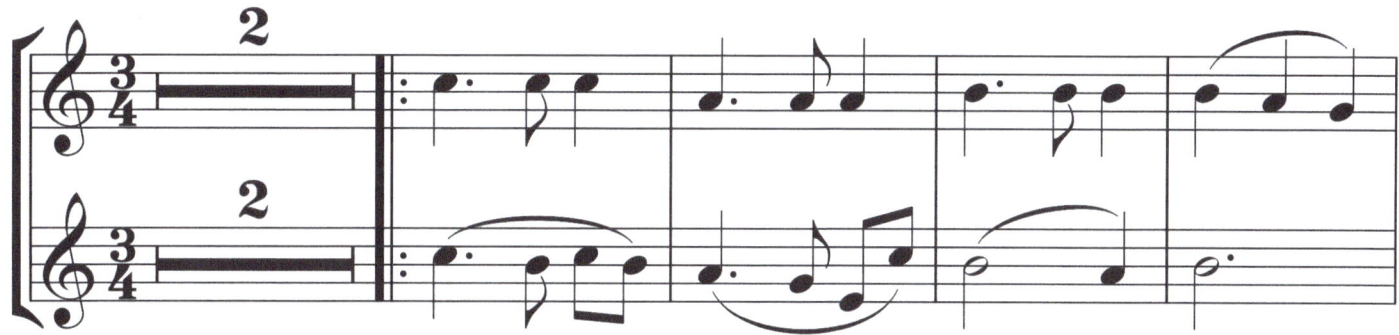

19. Jammin'

DGH

Wait for 6 bars introduction.

Improvise using E, G, F A, B, C, D until the end.

Stickers

www.ingramcontent.com/pod-product-compliance
Lightning Source LLC
Chambersburg PA
CBHW042144290426
44110CB00002B/110